To: Jenny

with love

From:

Chris Mc Arbor

This little book has meant
so much to me. I hope it
may bring some peace to you
also.

PRAYERS FOR INNER STRENGTH

Edited by
John Beilenson

Design by Michel Design

PETER PAUPER PRESS, INC.
WHITE PLAINS • NEW YORK

The Meaning of Prayer

THE WORD "prayer" in the Judeo-Christian tradition has two roots. In Latin the origin of the verb "to pray" is *precari,* meaning "to entreat." A prayer in this sense is an earnest request or petition, directed to God. In Hebrew, the verb "to pray"—*l'hit palael*—means literally to judge oneself. Prayer in this second sense is a meditation on how one measures up to God's teachings.

In this book, the reader will find both types of prayers—those that look up to God and those that look within. In times of need, specifically, the best prayers do not seek holy intervention but rather divine inspiration. They do not ask for miracles but for understanding of our problems in the broad perspective of God's purpose.

Prayers evolve from life situations. In difficult times, we look for words that speak most directly to our immediate problems.

Often, good prayers come not only from the Bible or a wise philosopher but from the heart of the person who prays. As we search ourselves for inspiration, we draw closer to God. In prayer, our inner turmoil is calmed by the nearness of God's serenity.

As Paul S. McElroy, a contemporary religious thinker states: "The thing to be sought [in prayer] is not how to get our way, but how to accept the will of God. The intent is not to change God's mind, but to change our attitudes. Prayer is really thinking in God's presence."

Let us give God an opportunity to do what He wants, through us. Let us pray!

J.B.

Prayers for the Bereaved

THE LORD IS MY SHEPHERD

THE LORD is my shepherd; I shall not want.
He maketh me to lie down in green pastures;
    he leadeth me beside the still waters.
He restoreth my soul; he leadeth me in the
    paths of righteousness for his name's sake.
Yea, though I walk through the valley of the
    shadow of death, I will fear no evil; for
    Thou art with me; Thy rod and Thy staff
    they comfort me.
Thou preparest a table before me in the
    presence of mine enemies; Thou anointest
    my head with oil; my cup runneth over.
Surely goodness and mercy shall follow me
    all the days of my life; and I will dwell in
    the house of the Lord for ever.

Psalm 23

IN THIS BITTER TRIAL

O G O D, help me to think of Thee in this bitter trial. Thou knowest how my heart is rent with grief. In my weakness, tested so severely in soul by this visitation, I cry unto Thee, Father of all life: give me fortitude to say with Thy servant Job: "The Lord hath given; the Lord hath taken away; blessed be the name of the Lord."

Forgive the thoughts of my rebellious soul. Pardon me in these first hours of my grief, if I question Thy wisdom and exercise myself in things too high for me. Grant me strength to rise above this trial, to bear with humility life's sorrows and disappointments. Be nigh unto me, O God. Bring consolation and peace to my soul. Praised art Thou, O God, who comfortest the mourners.

Union Prayer Book

A GRAIN OF SAND

A G R A I N of sand leads to the fall of a mountain when the moment has come for the mountain to fall.

Ernest Rena

THE BEGINNING OR THE END?

THERE is as much reason to assume that death is the beginning of a glorious adventure as to assume that it is the end of all. Surely, if a milligram of musk will give out perfume for seven thousand years, and a milligram of radium give out light for seventy thousand years, then the human soul, which is far more precious than musk or radium, will live for more than seventy years.

Paul S. McElroy

FOR THE LIFE OF THY FAITHFUL

FOR the life of thy faithful, O Lord, is changed, not destroyed [at death]; and when the home of this earthly life is dissolved, an everlasting dwelling in heaven shall be gained. Wherefore with the angels and archangels, with the thrones and dominions, with all the host of the army of heaven, we sing the hymn of thy glory, saying without end, Holy, Holy, Holy.

The Missal

WHY FEAR DEATH?

ALL men face what is inevitable. Why should death be feared? We begin to die as soon as we are born. At what moment, then, should we be most fearful of leaving the known for the unknown? Understandably, there may be a desire to postpone the transition—for ourselves and for our loved ones—but of what is there to be afraid?

Our physical body is lent to us as a house in which we live. When that dwelling becomes unfit for the purpose for which it was intended, a kind and benevolent nature has provided a way to get rid of that shell. That way is death.

Why then, should we be sad or rebellious? Death does bring changes and adjustments for those who are left behind. The warmth and association of former days are gone. The silence, the finality, the incommunicability disturb, but for our loved one who has triumphed, there should be rejoicing. Sorrow is centered on self.

Benjamin Franklin

THE ETERNAL GOODNESS

I LONG for household voices gone
For vanished smiles I long,
But God hath led my dear ones on
And He can do no wrong.

I know not what the future holds
Of marvel or surprise
Assured alone that life and death
His mercy underlies.

And so beside the silent sea
I wait the muffled oar;
No harm from Him can come to me
On ocean or on shore.

I know not where His islands lift
Their fronded palms in air;
I only know I cannot drift
Beyond His love and care.

John Greenleaf Whittier

THE DAWN HAS COME

DEATH is not extinguishing the light, but
putting out the lamp because the dawn has
come.

Rabindranath Tagore

ON THE DEATH OF A LOVED ONE

WE may reason bravely that our loved one
has lived to a ripe old age and we may be
relieved to know that his suffering is over at
last. We admit philosophically that death
has come as a blessing, but no matter what
our attitude may be, it hurts to lose a loved
one. Whether death has come after
prolonged illness in old age, or suddenly in
the prime of life, we must nevertheless be
grateful for the years we have been
privileged to be together, and for the joys
and sorrows that the relationship has
afforded.

Paul S. McElroy

FEEL THE MAJESTY OF GOD

WHATSOEVER praise we would render
unto God, howsoever we would adore the
Most High, we would yet fail Him the glory
due to His great Name. Even in the hour of
bereavement and sorrow, we feel the
majesty of God and will give thanks for His
manifold service.

Union Prayer Book

GUIDE US THROUGH THE DARKNESS

O THOU who art the strength of souls,
guide us through the darkness of this world,
guard us from its perils, hold us up and
strengthen us when we grow weary in our
mortal way, and lead us by thy chosen
paths, to our eternal home in thy heavenly
kingdom.

Hebrew Liturgy

THY NAME IN HEAVEN IS REST

THANK God for death!
Who touches anguished lips and
  stills their breath
And giveth peace unto each
  troubled breast;
Grief flies before thy touch,
  O blessed death;
God's sweetest gift; thy name
  in heaven is Rest.
  Thank God for death!

Unknown

LIVE WELL, LAUGH OFTEN, LOVE MUCH

HE HAS achieved success who has lived
well, laughed often and loved much; who
has gained the respect of intelligent men and
the love of little children; who has filled his
niche and accomplished his tasks; who has
left the world better than he found it,
whether by an improved poppy, a perfect
poem or a rescued soul; who has never
lacked appreciation of earth's beauty or
failed to express it; who has looked for the
best in others and given the best he had;
whose life was an inspiration; whose
memory is a benediction.

Mrs. Arthur J. Stanley

A PRAYER FOR MOURNERS

MAY the blessings of the Lord rest upon all
His people in every land, of every tongue.
The Lord meet in mercy all that seek Him.
The Lord comfort all that suffer and mourn.
The Lord hasten His coming, and give us
and all His people peace both now and forever
more.

War-Time Prayers

DEATH IS A FRIEND

DEATH is not the enemy of life, but its friend, for it is the knowledge that our years are limited which makes them so precious. It is the truth that time is but lent to us which makes us, at our best, look upon our years as a trust handed into our temporary keeping.

Paul S. McElroy

THE NATURE OF PRAYER

PRAYER does not change God, but changes him who prays.

Soren Kierkegaard

REJOICE IN SUFFERING

WE REJOICE in our sufferings, knowing that suffering produces endurance, and endurance produces character, and character produces hope, and hope does not disappoint us, because God's love has been poured into our hearts.

Romans: 5:3-5

OUT OF THE DARK A SHADOW

OUT of the dark a shadow,
  Then, a spark;
Out of the cloud a silence,
  Then, a lark;
Out of the heart a rapture,
  Then, a pain;
Out of the dead cold ashes,
  Life again.

John B. Tabb

NOT NEGLECTED

WE ought to be of good cheer in the face of
death and to hold firmly that this one thing,
at least, is true: no evil can come to a
righteous man either in life or in death, and
his interests are not neglected by the gods.

Socrates

Prayers for World Peace

WHEN PEACE SHALL REIGN

HOW BEAUTIFUL upon the mountains
are the feet of him that bringeth good
tidings, that publisheth peace; that bringeth
good tidings of good, that publisheth
salvation; that saith unto Zion, Thy God
reigneth! Thy watchmen shall lift up the
voice; with the voice together shall they
sing: for they shall see eye to eye, when the
Lord shall bring again Zion. Break forth
into joy, sing together, ye waste places of
Jerusalem: for the Lord hath comforted His
people, He hath redeemed Jerusalem. The
Lord hath made bare His holy arm in the
eyes of all the nations; and all the ends of
the earth shall see the salvation of our God.

Isaiah 52: 7-10

GIVE US PEACE

UNTO God's gracious mercy and protection we commit ourselves. The Lord bless us and keep us. The Lord make His face to shine upon us and be gracious unto us. The Lord lift up the light of His countenance upon us, and give us peace, both now and evermore.

Numbers 6:24-26

SEND PEACE UPON THE EARTH

O GOD our Father, on this Day of Remembrance, look upon the unrest of the world and be pleased to complete the work of Thy healing hand. Send peace upon the earth, a deeper and more lasting peace than the world has ever known. Draw all men unto Thyself, and to one another by the bands of love. Grant understanding to the Nations with an increase of sympathy and mutual good will, that they may be united in a sacred Brotherhood wherein justice, mercy and faith, truth and freedom may flourish, so that the sacrifice of those who died may not have been made in vain.

Paul S. McElroy

WE WILL NOT FEAR

G O D is our refuge and strength, a very present help in trouble. Therefore will not we fear, though the earth be removed, and though the mountains be carried into the midst of the sea; though the waters thereof roar and be troubled, though the mountains shake with the swelling thereof. Selah. There is a river, the streams whereof shall make glad the city of God, the holy place of the tabernacles of the Most High. God is in the midst of her; she shall not be moved: God shall help her, and that right early. The heathen raged, the kingdoms were moved: He uttered His voice, the earth melted. The Lord of hosts is with us; the God of Jacob is our refuge. Selah. Come, behold the works of the Lord, what desolations He hath made in the earth. He maketh wars to cease unto the end of the earth; He breaketh the bow, and cutteth the spear in sunder; He burneth the chariot in the fire. Be still, and know that I am God: I will be exalted among the heathen, I will be exalted in the earth. The Lord of hosts is with us; the God of Jacob is our refuge. Selah.

Psalm 46

WITH MALICE TOWARD NONE

WITH malice toward none; with charity
for all; with firmness in the right, as God
gives us to see the right, let us strive on to
finish the work we are in; to bind up the
nation's wounds; to care for him who shall
have borne the battle, and for his widow
and his orphan—to do all which may
achieve and cherish a just and lasting peace
among ourselves and with all nations.

Abraham Lincoln

SWORDS RATHER THAN OLIVE BRANCHES

THE LARGER power blocs of the world
talk passionately of pursuing peace while
burgeoning defense budgets bulge, enlarging
already awesome armies and devising even
more devastating weapons . . . The heads of
all of the nations issue clarion calls for
peace, yet these destiny defenders come
accompanied by a band and brigade of
national choristers, each bearing unsheathed
swords rather than olive branches.

Martin Luther King, Jr.

TEACH US PEACE

TEACH US, O Lord, to check in ourselves
and in others every temper which makes for
war, all ungenerous judgments, all
promptings of self-assertion, all
presumptuous claims; that being ever ready
to recognize the needs and aspirations of
other nations, we may, with patience, do
whatsoever in us lies to remove suspicions
and misunderstandings, and to honor all
men.

War-Time Prayers

SHOW US THY MERCY

LORD, Thou hast been favorable unto Thy
land: Thou has brought back the captivity
of Jacob. Thou hast forgiven the iniquity of
Thy people; Thou hast covered all their sin.
Selah. Thou hast taken away all Thy wrath:
Thou hast turned Thyself from the
fierceness of Thine anger. Turn us, O God
of our salvation, and cause Thine anger
toward us to cease. Wilt Thou be angry
with us forever? Wilt Thou draw out Thine
anger to all generations? Wilt Thou not
revive us again: that Thy people may rejoice

in Thee? Show us Thy mercy, O Lord, and grant us Thy salvation. I will hear what God the Lord will speak: for He will speak peace unto His people, and to His saints: but let them not turn again to folly. Surely His salvation is nigh them that fear Him; that glory may dwell in our land. Mercy and truth are met together; righteousness and peace have kissed each other. Truth shall spring out of the earth; and righteousness shall look down from heaven. Yea, the Lord shall give that which is good; and our land shall yield her increase. Righteousness shall go before Him; and shall set us in the way of His steps.

Psalm 85

A PRAYER TO END WAR

DISMAYED by the strife and jealousy which are bringing ruin to peoples and nations, we turn, O Jesus, to Thy most loving Heart as our only hope. O God of mercy, with tears we invoke Thee to end wars and the horror of war. O King of Peace, we humbly implore the peace for which we long.

Benedict XV

BLESSED IS THE PEACEMAKER

BLESSED is the peace-maker, not the
conqueror.

Ancient Proverb

THE SUPREME TRAGEDY OF THE BOMB

THE MORAL to be legitimately drawn
from the supreme tragedy of the bomb is
that it will not be destroyed by counter-
bombs even as violence can not be destroyed
by counter-violence. Mankind has to get out
of violence only through non-violence.
Hatred can only be overcome by love.

Mahatma Gandhi

SWORDS INTO PLOWSHARES

THEY shall beat their swords into
plowshares, and their spears into pruning
hooks; nation shall not lift up sword against
nation, neither shall they learn war any
more.

Isaiah 2:4

Prayers for the Sick

MORE THINGS ARE WROUGHT BY PRAYER

MORE things are wrought by prayer
Than this world dreams of. Wherefore, let
   thy voice
Rise like a fountain for me night
   and day.
For what are men better than
   sheep or goats
That nourish a blind life within
   the brain,
If, knowing God, they lift not
   hands of prayer
Both for themselves and those
   who call them friends?

Alfred, Lord Tennyson

LET IT BLESS YOU

ADVERSITY and misfortune may handicap us in various ways, but there are many things we can do in spite of limitations. It is what we can do and not what we cannot that counts. In spite of setbacks there is still much that we can do. Many disabled people accomplish far more than do non-disadvantaged people. The secret of success lies in the will to do. The opportunity for achievement is still open to the less-privileged, provided they have sufficient determination to make the most of circumstances. The writer of the Book of Genesis records the words which Jacob allegedly uttered when he wrestled with the "angel" at Peniel. Even though the struggle caused Jacob to limp throughout his life, he did not give up, but exclaimed with profound insight, "I will not let thee go until thou bless me." With Jacob, we can resolve not to let unfavorable experiences go until they bless us.

Paul S. McElroy

IF YOUR LEGS FAIL, FIGHT ON YOUR KNEES

THE ESTIMATE and valor of a man consists in the heart and in the will; there his true honor lies. Valor is stability, not of arms and legs, but of courage and the soul; it does not lie in the valor of our horse, nor of our arms, but in ourselves. He that falls obstinate in his courage, if his legs fail him, fights upon his knees.

Michel De Montaigne

GOD WILL SUSTAIN YOU

CAST your burdens on the Lord, and He will sustain you.

Psalm 55:22

LAY ME DOWN IN PEACE

I WILL lay me down in peace and take my rest, for it is Thou, Lord, only that makest me dwell in safety.

Psalm 4:8

UNTIL WE LEARN TO SING THY SONG

O LORD our God, when the storm is loud, and the night is dark, and the soul is sad, and the heart oppressed; then, as weary travelers, may we look to Thee; and beholding the light of Thy love, may it bear us on, until we learn to sing Thy song in the night.

George Dawson

ONE VIEW OF DEATH

I HAVE fought a good fight, I have often faltered, but I have kept up the race. I have been besieged all my life with doubts, but I have kept my faith. I look forward to the great adventure with awe, but not with apprehension. I have enjoyed my work, my home, my friends, my life—I shall be sorry to part with them. But always I have stood in the bow looking forward with hopeful anticipation to the life before me. When the time comes for my embarkation and I put out to sea, I think I shall still be standing in the bow looking forward with eager curiosity.

Lyman Abbott

THE STRENGTH OF SUFFERING

ALMIGHTY and everlasting God, the
Comfort of the sad, the Strength of
sufferers, let the prayers of those that cry
out of any tribulation come unto Thee, that
all may rejoice to find that Thy mercy is
present with them in their afflictions.

Fifth Century

GRANT US RELIEF

O GOD, our Refuge in pain, our Strength
in weakness, our Help in trouble, we come
to Thee in our hour of need, beseeching
Thee to have mercy upon this Thine
afflicted servant. O loving Father, relieve
his pain. Yet if he needs must suffer,
strengthen him, that he may bear his
sufferings with patience and as his day is, so
may his strength be. Let not his heart be
troubled, but shed down upon him the peace
which passeth understanding. Though now
for a season, if need be, he is in heaviness
through his manifold trials, yet comfort
him, O Lord, in all his sorrows, and let his
mourning be turned into joy, and his
sickness into health.

E.B. Pusey

BE NOT DISMAYED

H A R D S H I P and disappointment, physical
pain and mental suffering may come in life,
but that does not mean that God is
deserting us, nor does it mean that God is
punishing us. God may love, yet not spare
us from misfortune. The important thing is
to know that no matter what happens God
will care for us. "Be not afraid, neither be
dismayed, for the Lord your God is with
you where ever you may go."

Paul S. McElroy

GIVE US COURAGE

G I V E U S courage, gaiety and the quiet
mind. Spare to us our friends, soften to us
our enemies. Bless us, if it may be, in all
our innocent endeavors. If it may not, give
us the strength to encounter that which is
to come, that we be brave in peril, constant
in tribulation, temperate in wrath, and in all
changes of fortune and down to the gates of
death, loyal and loving one to another.

Robert Louis Stevenson

THE PEACE OF GOD

GRANT unto us, Almighty God, the peace of God that passeth understanding, that we, amid the storms and troubles of this our life, may rest in Thee, knowing that all things are in Thee; not beneath Thine eye only, but under Thy care, governed by Thy will, guarded by Thy love, so that with a quiet heart we may see the storms of life, the cloud and the thick darkness, ever rejoicing to know that the darkness and the light are both alike to Thee. Guide, guard, and govern us even to the end, that none of us may fail to lay hold upon the immortal life.

George Dawson

SING HYMNS TO GOD

WHAT else can I, a lame old man, do but sing hymns to God? If I were a nightingale I would act the part of a nightingale, if a swan, the part of a swan, but since I am a reasonable creature, it is my duty to praise God. This is my business, I do it. . . .

Epictetus

33

IN SPITE OF HANDICAPS

W H Y does not God grant to unusually
gifted people the advantage of good health?
Why are talented people often limited in the
expression of their gifts by physical
handicaps and sickness? The answer may be
in the fact that sickness does not destroy
one's talents; it may merely make it more
difficult for one to execute his task. A
handicap often sharpens one's powers and
prompts one to do things he could not have
achieved, if he had been well.

Beethoven was deaf; John Keats,
Elizabeth Barrett Browning, Sidney Lanier,
Chopin, Robert Louis Stevenson, and
Thoreau were all tubercular; President
Roosevelt was a victim of poliomyelitis. Yet
illness was not allowed to hinder them.
These people admittedly may have
accomplished more with full health, but is it
not also possible that their contributions
could be made because of handicaps? Who
knows but that their misfortunes gave them
deeper insight and understanding?

Paul S. McElroy

BURN OUR OWN SMOKE

THE FIRST lesson of life is to burn our own smoke; that is, not to inflict on outsiders our personal sorrows and petty morbidness, not to keep thinking of ourselves as exceptional cases.

James Russell Lowell

GOD AT WORK IN ADVERSITY

NYDIA, the blind flower girl in Bulwer-Lytton's *The Last Days of Pompeii,* a sad and pitiful figure, moves through the story, groping her way unerringly about the winding streets of Pompeii. When Vesuvius buries the city in molten lava, all is in total darkness and terror-stricken inhabitants rush frantically to and fro in an effort to escape. They are lost in the awful blackness. But Nydia, accustomed as she is to the dark, goes swiftly through the streets and rescues the one she loves. If only we could know for what our crosses may be fitting us! God may be at work in us in times of darkness.

Paul S. McElroy

A BLESSING FOR THE SICK

YOU know, O Lord, the concerns, the feelings, the anxieties of mankind. Bless them. Bless those who are victims of illnesses they strive to conquer. Bless those who have fallen from grace and whose burdens are beyond their strength to bear. Open my eyes to possibilities that are hidden. Enlarge my heart that I may hold in my prayers the hopes and fears of those who need me and of those who long to know you.

Paul S. McElroy

GONE WHERE?

IMAGINE you are standing on the seashore. A ship at your side spreads her white sails to the morning breeze and starts for the blue ocean. She is an object of beauty and strength and you stand and watch her until at length she hangs like a speck of white cloud just where the sea and sky meet and mingle with each other: "There, she is gone."

Gone where? Gone from your sight, that is all. She is just as large in hull and mast and spar as when she left your side and just as able to bear her load of living freight to the place of her destination. Her diminished size is in you, not in her.

And just at the moment when someone at your side says, "She's gone," there are other eyes watching for her coming and other voices ready to take up the glad shout, "Here she comes!" And this is what we call dying—this is life!

Paul S. McElroy

THE WORTH OF LIFE

H E L P me, O God, to learn from Thee that the worth of life depends not upon the years of its duration, but on the spirit in which it is lived.

Paul S. McElroy

AFFLICTED BUT NOT CRUSHED

W E A R E afflicted in every way, but not crushed; perplexed, but not driven to despair; persecuted, but not forsaken; struck down, but not destroyed.

II Corinthians 4:8-9

Prayers for
Inner Peace

FROM WHENCE DOES MY HELP COME?

I LIFT up my eyes to the hills.
  From whence does my help come?
My help comes from the Lord,
  Who made heaven and earth.

He will not let your foot be moved,
  He who keeps you will not slumber.
Behold, he who keeps Israel
  will neither slumber nor sleep.

The Lord is your keeper;
  the Lord is your shade on your
  right hand.
The sun shall not smite you by day,
  nor the moon by night.

The Lord will keep you from all evil;
  He will keep your life.
The Lord will keep your going out
  and your coming in from this time
  forth and for evermore.

Psalm 121

LOOK AROUND

JUST as the hand, held before the eye, can hide the tallest mountain, so the routine of everyday life can keep us from seeing the vast radiance and the secret wonders that fill the world.

Hasidic, 18th Century

LET DEFEAT TEACH ANEW

ALMIGHTY Father, Source of all blessings, we thank Thee for the preservation of our life and for the joy of living, for the powers of mind and heart and for the wisdom that comes to us from seers and sages filled with Thy spirit.

Teach us to use wisely the blessings Thou hast bestowed upon us. May prosperity not enfeeble our spirit nor harden our heart. May it never so master us as to dull our desire for life's higher ideals.
And should adversity come, may it not embitter us nor cause us to despair, but may we accept it as a mark of Thy chastening

love which purifies and strengthens. Let
every obstacle become an incentive to
greater effort, and let every defeat teach us
anew the lesson of patience and
perseverance.

Gird us with strength to bear our trials with
courage. Let not the loss of anything,
however dear to our hearts or precious in
our sight, rob us of our faith in Thee. In
light as in darkness, in joy as in sorrow,
help us to put our trust in Thy providence,
that even through our tears we may discern
Thy divine blessing.

Union Prayer Book

GOD IS FAITHFUL

G O D is faithful and will not suffer you to
be tempted above that you are able.

I Corinthians 10:13

AFTER WINTER, SPRING

I F W I N T E R comes, can Spring be far
behind?

Percy Bysshe Shelley

NEVER LOSE COURAGE

HE WHO loses wealth loses much; he who loses a friend loses more; but he that loses his courage loses all.

Miguel De Cervantes

GIVE ME SERENITY

O GOD, give me the serenity to accept what cannot be changed—
Give me the courage to change what can be changed—
And the wisdom to know the one from the other. Amen.

Reinhold Niebuhr

THE MOST DURABLE POWER

LOVE is the most durable power in the world. This creative force, so beautifully exemplified in the life of Christ, is the most potent instrument available in mankind's quest for peace and security.

Martin Luther King, Jr.

ADVERSITY IS A TRUE FRIEND

A HIGH character might be produced, I suppose, by continued prosperity, but it has very seldom been the case. Adversity, however it may appear to be our foe, is our true friend; and, after a little acquaintance with it, we receive it as a precious thing— the prophecy of a coming joy. It should be no ambition of ours to traverse a path without a thorn or stone.

Charles H. Spurgeon

DELIVER US, O LORD

O GOD, our help in ages past, our hope today and forever, have mercy upon humanity in its blindness, its bitterness, and its confusion. Deliver us, O Lord, from lust of power, from vanity of spirit, from envy, apathy, and ill-will. Touch our minds with light, that, having a right understanding, we may have compassion, and courage, and patience—working with Thy help for the better order of the ages.

Source Unknown

LIFT UP MY SOUL

LET ME not seek out of Thee what I can find only in Thee, O Lord, peace and rest and joy and bliss, which abide only in Thine abiding joy. Lift up my soul above the weary round or harassing thoughts to Thy eternal Presence. Lift up my soul to the pure, bright, serene, radiant atmosphere of Thy Presence, that there I may breathe freely, there repose in Thy love, there be at rest from myself, and from all things that weary me; and thence return, arrayed with Thy peace, to do and bear what shall please Thee.

E.B. Pusey

THE NECESSITY OF SORROW

Who never broke with tears, his
    bread,
Who never watched through
    anguished hours
With weeping eyes, upon his bed,
He knows ye not, O Heavenly
    Powers.

Goethe

STOP WORRYING

SOME of your hurts have cured,
And the sharpest you still have
   survived,
But what torments of grief you
   endured
From evils that never arrived.

                    Ralph Waldo Emerson

IMITATE GOD

IN CONNECTION with the Mitzvah
[duty] of following the right path, it has
been taught: As God is called gracious, so
must you be gracious; as God is
compassionate, so must you be; as God is
holy, so must you follow the path of
holiness. Therefore the prophets described
God as possessing these attributes: endlessly
patient and loving, just and upright,
wholehearted, and the like. Their intention
was to teach us that these are the good and
praiseworthy paths for us to follow as we
attempt, according to our capacities, to
imitate God.

                    Maimonides, 12th Century

PRAYER FOR A DREARY DAY

GOD of our life, there are days when the burdens we carry chafe our shoulders and weigh us down; when the road seems dreary and endless, the skies grey and threatening; when our lives have no music in them, and our hearts are lonely, and our souls have lost their courage. Flood the path with light, we beseech Thee; turn our eyes to where the skies are full of promise; tune our hearts to brave music; give us the sense of comradeship with heroes and saints of every age; and so quicken our spirits that we may be able to encourage the souls of all who journey with us on the road to life, to Thy honor and glory.

St. Augustine

PROVIDED THE HEART IS RIGHT

WE shall steer safely through every storm,
    so long as our heart is right,
Our intention fervent, our courage
steadfast,
    and our trust fixed on God.

St. Francis De Sales

GIVE ME FAITH

GIVE me, O Lord, a steadfast heart, which no unworthy affection may drag downwards; give me an unconquered heart, which no tribulation can wear out; give me an upright heart, which no unworthy purpose may tempt aside.

Thomas Aquinas

NOTHING TO FEAR

SO, IN REGARD to disagreeable and formidable things, prudence does not consist in evasion or flight, but in courage. He who wishes to walk in the most peaceful parts of life with any serenity must screw himself up to resolution. Let him front the object of his worst apprehension, and his stoutness will commonly make his fear groundless.

Ralph Waldo Emerson

FROM THE LOWLIEST DEPTH

FROM the lowliest depth there is a path to the loftiest height.

William Carlyle

THE ONLY FAILURE

THE ONLY failure a man ought to fear is failure in cleaving to the purpose he sees to be best.

George Eliot

SUFFERING IS NOT PUNISHMENT FOR SIN

IN ADDITION to physical pain, hardship, and mental anxiety, many people carry an enormous burden of guilt because, like Job's accusers, they feel that suffering is inflicted as punishment for sin, which, knowingly or unwittingly, has been committed.

Whenever a person breaks a law deliberately or inadvertently, somebody is hurt, damage is done, and a price must be paid. But there is consolation in the fact that suffering may be the consequence of wrong-doing rather than punishment for wrong-doing. Suffering is not imposed upon one by a jealous and revengeful God. A kind, benevolent God may allow His people to suffer, but this is quite different from assuming that God is sadistically imposing hardship.

Paul S. McElroy

A PRAYER TO START THE DAY

O LORD, support us all day long, until the shadows lengthen and the evening comes, and the busy world is hushed and the fever of life is over, and our work is done. Then in thy mercy grant us a safe lodging and a holy rest and peace at the last. Amen.

John Henry Newman

A LESSON FROM HISTORY

WHEN it gets darkest, the stars come
    out.
When a bee steals from a flower,
    it also fertilizes that flower.
Whom the gods would destroy, they
    first make mad.
The mills of the gods grind slowly,
    but they grind exceedingly fine.

Charles A. Beard

AN ENCOURAGING FACT

I KNOW of no more encouraging fact than the unquestionable ability of man to elevate his life by a conscious endeavor.

Henry David Thoreau

RISE ABOVE NARROW CONFINES

AN INDIVIDUAL has not started living until he can rise above the narrow confines of his individual concerns to the broader concerns of all humanity.

Martin Luther King, Jr.

BRING US UNTO THY REST

O LORD, who art as the shadow of a great rock in a weary land, who beholdest Thy weak creatures, weary of labor, weary of pleasure, weary of hope deferred, weary of self, in Thine abundant compassion and unutterable tenderness, bring us unto Thy rest.

Christina Rossetti

DEFEND US

O GOD, by Thy mercy strengthen us who lie exposed to the rough storms of troubles and temptations. Help us against our own negligence and cowardice, and defend us from the treachery of our unfaithful hearts. Succor us, we beseech Thee, and bring us to Thy safe haven of peace and felicity.

Thomas a Kempis

THE GLORY OF THE LATE DAYS

WE THANK Thee, Lord, for the glory of
the late days and the excellent face of Thy
sun. We thank Thee for good news
received. We thank Thee for the pleasures
we have enjoyed and for those we have been
able to confer. And now, when the clouds
gather and the rain impends, permit us not
to be cast down; let us not lose the savor of
past mercies and past pleasures; but, like
the voice of a bird singing in the rain, let
grateful memory survive in the hour of
darkness. If there be in front of us any
painful duty, strengthen us with the grace
of courage; if any act of mercy, teach us
tenderness and patience.

Robert Louis Stevenson

VIRTUE IN ENDURANCE

BLESSED is the man who endures trial,
for when he has stood the test, he will
receive the crown of life which God has
promised to those who love Him.

James 1:12

THANK GOD FOR WORK

THANK God every morning when you get up that you have something to do which must be done, whether you like it or not. Being forced to work, and forced to do your best, will breed in you temperance, self-control, diligence, strength of will, content, and a hundred other virtues which the idle never know.

Charles Kingsley

BE NOT AFRAID

BE STRONG and of a good courage; be not afraid, neither be thou dismayed: for the Lord thy God is with thee whithersoever thou goest.

Joshua 1:9

A STEPPING STONE

THE BLOCK of granite which is an obstacle in the pathway of the weak, becomes a stepping stone in the pathway of the strong.

Thomas Carlyle

PRAY NOT

PRAY not! The darkness will not
   brighter be!
Nought ask the silence, for it
   cannot speak!
Nought from the helpless gods by
   gift and hymn,
Within yourselves deliverance must
   be sought.
Nor bribe with blood, nor feed with
   fruit and cakes.

Japanese (Buddhist), First Century B.C.

THE HAND OF GOD

ON THE OUTSKIRTS of the desert
where village life goes along much as it did
centuries ago, an eclipse of the moon
occurred. As the shadow crept across the
face of the moon, the residents were asked
what was happening. Some replied that the
moon was only sinking behind a mountain;
others claimed it was merely the quarter
phase of the moon; still others said it was
hiding behind a cloud; but one old village

54

sheikh, undisturbed by the growing darkness, imaginatively assured the onlookers that the phenomenon was the hand of God covering the moon. To be able to see the hand of God at work in the world is one of the greatest assets one can have. When the shadows are gathering for life's darker moments, the person who can still see God's hand at work, even in unfavorable circumstances, will be master of any situation life may impose upon him.

Paul S. McElroy

A MORNING PRAYER

WE THANK Thee, O Lord our God, for all Thy goodness. Thou hast shielded, rescued, helped, and guided us all the days of our lives, and brought us unto this hour. Grant in Thy goodness that we may spend this day without sin, in joy and reverence of Thee. Drive away from us all envy, all fear. Bestow upon us what is good and meet. And lead us not into temptation, but deliver us from evil.

Unknown.

STRENGTHEN OUR HEARTS

O GOD, keep my tongue from evil and my lips from speaking guile. Be my support when grief silences my voice, and my comfort when woe bends my spirit. Plant humility in my soul, and strengthen my heart with perfect faith in Thee. Help me to be strong in trial and temptation and to be meek when others wrong me, that I may readily forgive them. Guide me by the light of Thy counsel, and let me ever find rest in Thee, who are my Rock and my Redeemer. Let the words of my mouth and the meditation of my heart be acceptable in Thy sight, O Lord, my Rock and my Redeemer.

Union Prayer Book

TESTING PRODUCES STEADFASTNESS

COUNT it all joy when you meet various trials, for you know that the testing of your faith produces steadfastness. And let your steadfastness have its full effect, that you may be perfect and complete, lacking in nothing.

James 1:2-4

A SOUL'S REFUGE

O THOU full of compassion, I commit and commend myself unto Thee, in whom I am, and live, and know. Be Thou the Goal of my pilgrimage, and my Rest by the way. Let my soul take refuge from the crowding turmoil of worldly thought beneath the shadow of Thy wings; let my heart, this sea of restless waves, find peace in Thee, O God.

St. Augustine

OPEN OUR EYES

HEAVENLY Father, in whom is no darkness at all, nor any shadow that is cast by turning, forgive our feverish ways—our anxieties, our fears, our uncertainties. We are like children walking wilfully and blindly in darkness while the world without is ablaze with light. Open our eyes that we may see Thee; and our minds that we may understand and know Thee. Help us to make the great adventure of faith, and discover the secret of peace, in finding Thee, Thou great Companion of our souls.

Prayers for Faith and Trust

THE STRENGTH OF GOD

M A Y the strength of God pilot us. May the power of God preserve us. May the wisdom of God instruct us. May the hand of God protect us. May the way of God direct us. May the shield of God defend us.

May the host of God guard us against the snares of the Evil One and the temptations of the world.

Saint Patrick

COURAGE

C O U R A G E! Suffering, when it climbs highest, lasts not long.

Aeschylus

MAKING A GAME OF DIFFICULTY

M A U R I C E R A V E L, afflicted by insomnia, fatigue, and occasional amnesia, was approached in 1929 to write a piano concerto for the one-armed pianist, Paul Wittgenstein. Ravel created the now famous

58

Concerto for the Left Hand Alone. Ravel
remarked to Wittgenstein regarding their
handicaps, "I make a game of difficulty."

Paul S. McElroy

WATCH OVER ME

P R A I S E D be Thou, O God, who dost
make the day bright with Thy sunshine, and
the night with the beams of heavenly fires.
Listen now to my prayers; watch over me
with Thy power; give me grace to pass all
the days of my life blamelessly, free from
sin and terror. For with Thee is mercy and
plenteous redemption, O Lord, my God.

Liturgy of Greek Church

A VERY PRESENT HELP

G O D is our refuge and strength, a very
present help in time of trouble.

Psalm 46:1

GOD'S HELP

GOD helps the brave.

Johann Von Schiller

A BLESSING IN DISGUISE

MISFORTUNE of any kind is pretty discouraging. It usually causes one to change his plans radically. A person can give in or give up. One may need, as a result, to seek a new vocation, but there is hope in the possibility that one may be more successful and more useful in the new vocation than he could have been in the old. Braille was trained as a cobbler, but an awl slipped and blinded him. As a result he developed the Braille system of reading for the blind.

It is also true that a handicap may make one more determined than ever to succeed and even excel. Glenn Cunningham, in spite of a serious burn on the leg, became the world's fastest miler.

There is consolation in the fact that what one regards as a misfortune may prove to be a blessing in disguise.

Paul S. McElroy

THE ABUNDANCE OF THY MERCY

ALMIGHTY and everlasting God, Who art always more ready to hear than we to pray, and art wont to give more than either we desire or deserve, pour down upon us the abundance of Thy mercy, forgiving us those things whereof our conscience is afraid, and giving us those things which we are not worthy to ask.

Leonine Sacramentary

GIVE US STRENGTH

WE BESEECH Thee, our most gracious God, preserve us from the cares of this life, lest we should be too much entangled therein; also from the many necessities of the body, lest we should be ensnared by pleasure; and from whatsoever is an obstacle to the soul, lest, being broken with troubles, we should be overthrown. Give us strength to resist, patience to endure, and constancy to persevere.

Thomas a Kempis

For Mom and Dad,
The Second Generation
Copyright © 1986
Peter Pauper Press, Inc.
202 Mamaroneck Avenue
White Plains, NY 10601
ISBN 0-88088-468-1
Printed in Hong Kong
7   6   5   4   3   2   1